This Christmas Recipe Book Belongs to

....

Contents Page	
Recipe Number	Recipe
Recipe 1	
Recipe 2	
Recipe 3	
Recipe 4	
Recipe 5	
Recipe 6	
Recipe 7	
Recipe 8	
Recipe 9	
Recipe 10	
Recipe 11	
Recipe 12	
Recipe 13	
Recipe 14	
Recipe 15	
Recipe 16	
Recipe 17	
Recipe 18	
Recipe 19	
Recipe 20	

Contents Page	
Recipe Number	Recipe
Recipe 21	
Recipe 22	
Recipe 23	
Recipe 24	
Recipe 25	
Recipe 26	
Recipe 27	
Recipe 28	
Recipe 29	
Recipe 30	
Recipe 31	
Recipe 32	
Recipe 33	
Recipe 34	
Recipe 35	
Recipe 36	
Recipe 37	
Recipe 38	
Recipe 39	
Recipe 40	

Contents Page

Recipe Number	Recipe
Recipe 41	
Recipe 42	
Recipe 43	
Recipe 44	
Recipe 45	
Recipe 46	
Recipe 47	
Recipe 48	
Recipe 49	
Recipe 50	
Recipe 51	
Recipe 52	
Recipe 53	
Recipe 54	
Recipe 55	
Recipe 56	
Recipe 57	
Recipe 58	
Recipe 59	
Recipe 60	

Contents Page

Recipe Number	Recipe
Recipe 61	
Recipe 62	
Recipe 63	
Recipe 64	
Recipe 65	
Recipe 66	
Recipe 67	
Recipe 68	
Recipe 69	
Recipe 70	
Recipe 71	
Recipe 72	
Recipe 73	
Recipe 74	
Recipe 75	
Recipe 76	
Recipe 77	
Recipe 78	
Recipe 79	
Recipe 80	

Contents Page

Recipe Number	Recipe
Recipe 81	
Recipe 82	
Recipe 83	
Recipe 84	
Recipe 85	
Recipe 86	
Recipe 87	
Recipe 88	
Recipe 89	
Recipe 90	
Recipe 91	
Recipe 92	
Recipe 93	
Recipe 94	
Recipe 95	
Recipe 96	
Recipe 97	
Recipe 98	
Recipe 99	
Recipe 100	

Recipe 1:

Ingredients:

Method:

Notes:

Recipe 2:

Ingredients:

Method:

Notes:

Recipe 3:

Ingredients:

Method:

Notes:

Recipe 4:

Ingredients:

Method:

Notes:

Recipe 5:

Ingredients:

Method:

Notes:

Recipe 6:

Ingredients:

Method:

Notes:

Recipe 7:

Ingredients:

Method:

Notes:

Recipe 8:

Ingredients:

Method:

Notes:

Recipe 9:

Ingredients:

Method:

Notes:

Recipe 10:

Ingredients:

Method:

Notes:

Recipe 11:

Ingredients:

Method:

Notes:

Recipe 12:

Ingredients:

Method:

Notes:

Recipe 13:

Ingredients:

Method:

Notes:

Recipe 14:

Ingredients:

Method:

Notes:

Recipe 15:

Ingredients:

Method:

Notes:

Recipe 16:

Ingredients:

Method:

Notes:

Recipe 17:

Ingredients:

Method:

Notes:

Recipe 18:

Ingredients:

Method:

Notes:

Recipe 19:

Ingredients:

Method:

Notes:

Recipe 20:

Ingredients:

Method:

Notes:

Recipe 21:

Ingredients:

Method:

Notes:

Recipe 22:

Ingredients:

Method:

Notes:

Recipe 23:

Ingredients:

Method:

Notes:

Recipe 24:

Ingredients:

Method:

Notes:

Recipe 25:

Ingredients:

Method:

Notes:

Recipe 26:

Ingredients:

Method:

Notes:

Recipe 27:

Ingredients:

Method:

Notes:

Recipe 28:

Ingredients:

Method:

Notes:

Recipe 29:

Ingredients:

Method:

Notes:

Recipe 30:

Ingredients:

Method:

Notes:

Recipe 31:

Ingredients:

Method:

Notes:

Recipe 32:

Ingredients:

Method:

Notes:

Recipe 33:

Ingredients:

Method:

Notes:

Recipe 34:

Ingredients:

Method:

Notes:

Recipe 35:

Ingredients:

Method:

Notes:

Recipe 36:

Ingredients:

Method:

Notes:

Recipe 37:

Ingredients:

Method:

Notes:

Recipe 38:

Ingredients:

Method:

Notes:

Recipe 39:

Ingredients:

Method:

Notes:

Recipe 40:

Ingredients:

Method:

Notes:

Recipe 41:

Ingredients:

Method:

Notes:

Recipe 42:

Ingredients:

Method:

Notes:

Recipe 43:

Ingredients:

Method:

Notes:

Recipe 44:

Ingredients:

Method:

Notes:

Recipe 45:

Ingredients:

Method:

Notes:

Recipe 46:

Ingredients:

Method:

Notes:

Recipe 47:

Ingredients:

Method:

Notes:

Recipe 48:

Ingredients:

Method:

Notes:

Recipe 49:

Ingredients:

Method:

Notes:

Recipe 50:

Ingredients:

Method:

Notes:

Recipe 51:

Ingredients:

Method:

Notes:

Recipe 52:

Ingredients:

_____   _____   _____

_____   _____   _____

_____   _____   _____

Method:

Notes:

Recipe 53:

Ingredients:

Method:

Notes:

Recipe 54:

Ingredients:

Method:

Notes:

Recipe 55:

Ingredients:

Method:

Notes:

Recipe 56:

Ingredients:

Method:

Notes:

Recipe 57:

Ingredients:

Method:

Notes:

Recipe 58:

Ingredients:

Method:

Notes:

Recipe 59:

Ingredients:

Method:

Notes:

Recipe 60:

Ingredients:

Method:

Notes:

Recipe 61:

Ingredients:

Method:

Notes:

Recipe 62:

Ingredients:

Method:

Notes:

Recipe 63:

Ingredients:

Method:

Notes:

Recipe 64:

Ingredients:

Method:

Notes:

Recipe 65:

Ingredients:

Method:

Notes:

Recipe 66:

Ingredients:

Method:

Notes:

Recipe 67:

Ingredients:

Method:

Notes:

Recipe 68:

Ingredients:

Method:

Notes:

Recipe 69:

Ingredients:

Method:

Notes:

Recipe 70:

Ingredients:

Method:

Notes:

Recipe 71:

Ingredients:

Method:

Notes:

Recipe 72:

Ingredients:

Method:

Notes:

Recipe 73:

Ingredients:

Method:

Notes:

Recipe 74:

Ingredients:

Method:

Notes:

Recipe 75:

Ingredients:

Method:

Notes:

Recipe 76:

Ingredients:

Method:

Notes:

Recipe 77:

Ingredients:

Method:

Notes:

Recipe 78:

Ingredients:

Method:

Notes:

Recipe 79:

Ingredients:

Method:

Notes:

Recipe 80:

Ingredients:

Method:

Notes:

Recipe 81:

Ingredients:

Method:

Notes:

Recipe 82:

Ingredients:

Method:

Notes:

Recipe 83:

Ingredients:

Method:

Notes:

Recipe 84:

Ingredients:

Method:

Notes:

Recipe 85:

Ingredients:

Method:

Notes:

Recipe 86:

Ingredients:

Method:

Notes:

Recipe 87:

Ingredients:

Method:

Notes:

Recipe 88:

Ingredients:

Method:

Notes:

Recipe 89:

Ingredients:

Method:

Notes:

Recipe 90:

Ingredients:

Method:

Notes:

Recipe 91:

Ingredients:

Method:

Notes:

Recipe 92:

Ingredients:

Method:

Notes:

Recipe 93:

Ingredients:

Method:

Notes:

Recipe 94:

Ingredients:

Method:

Notes:

Recipe 95:

Ingredients:

Method:

Notes:

Recipe 96:

Ingredients:

Method:

Notes:

Recipe 97:

Ingredients:

Method:

Notes:

Recipe 98:

Ingredients:

Method:

Notes:

Recipe 99:

Ingredients:

Method:

Notes:

Recipe 100:

Ingredients:

Method:

Notes:

Printed in Great Britain
by Amazon